THE OLYMPICS
EVENTS

THE OLYMPICS
EVENTS

Moira Butterfield

W
FRANKLIN WATTS
LONDON • SYDNEY

First published in 2011 by Franklin Watts

Copyright © Franklin Watts 2011

Franklin Watts
338 Euston Road
London NW1 3BH

Franklin Watts Australia
Level 17/207 Kent Street
Sydney, NSW 2000

A CIP catalogue record for this book
is available from the British Library.

Dewey number: 796.4'8

ISBN: 978 1 4451 0271 9

Printed in China.

Franklin Watts is a division of Hachette Children's Books, an Hachette UK company

www.hachette.co.uk

Series editor: Sarah Ridley
Editor in chief: John C. Miles
Designer: Jason Billin
Art director: Jonathan Hair
Picture research: Diana Morris

Picture credits: Allsport/Getty Images: 26. Robert Beck/Sports Illustrated/Getty Images: 11b. Alessandro dell Bella/epa/Corbis: 22c. Greg Breloer/Corbis: 5. Mark Dadswell/Getty Images: 10. Fred Dufour/AFP/Getty Images: 24t. Don Emmert/AFP/Getty Images: 24b. Chris Faytok/Star Ledger/Corbis: 22b. Julian Finney/Getty Images: 27. Guo Lei/Xinhua Press/Corbis: 21. Julian Herbert/Getty Images: 12, 13. Jo Yong-Hak/Reuters/Corbis: 16b. Jung Keon-Je/AFP/Getty Images: 19t. Streeter Lecka/Getty Images: 3, 18. Liu Dawei/Xinhua/Corbis: 8. Alex Livesey/Getty Images: 28. Kat Nietfeld/epa/Corbis: 9. Professional Sport/Topfoto: 15t, 19c. Quinn Rooney/Getty Images: 11t, 14. Sampics/Corbis: 17. Erich Schlegel/Dallas Morning News/Corbis: 16c. Carl de Souza/AFP/Getty Images: 15c. Jamie Squire/Getty Images: front cover. Matthew Stockman/Getty Images: 29. Al Tielemans/Sports Illustrated/Getty Images: 7. Ullsteinbild/Topfoto: 6, 20. Manan Vatsyayana/AFP/Getty Images: 25. Xu Jiajun/Xinhua/Corbis: 23.

Every attempt has been made to clear copyright. Should there be any inadvertent omission please apply to the publisher for rectification.

Note to parents and teachers

Every effort has been made by the Publishers to ensure that the websites in this book are suitable for children, that they are of the highest educational value, and that they contain no inappropriate or offensive material. However, because of the nature of the Internet, it is impossible to guarantee that the contents of these sites will not be altered. We strongly advise that Internet access is supervised by a responsible adult.

CONTENTS

Downloadable activity
and information sheets
are available at
www.franklinwatts.co.uk

The Summer Olympic Games are held every four years, and showcase the fastest, strongest and most skilful sportspeople on the planet. The world's swiftest runners compete in the track events, held in and around the Olympic Stadium.

The fastest races – the 100 metres (m), 200 m and 400 m – are called sprints. They are over in just a few exciting seconds. The runners start from blocks and must stay in eight numbered lanes marked on the track. The starting gun and the blocks are fitted with sensors, and if they detect that a runner has started less than 0.1 seconds after the gun is fired, it counts as a false start. To win, runners must get their torso (the body between the head to waist) across the line first.

Middle- and long-distance events
The 800 m and 1,500 m are called 'middle-distance' races. The 5,000 m and 10,000 m are called 'long-distance' races. The athletes begin a race spread across

Jamaican record-breaker Usain Bolt prepares himself before the final of the Beijing men's 100 m sprint in 2008.

6

staggered lanes – the ones in the outer lanes begin further forward to compensate for the bends in the track. Then, after a certain distance, all the competitors are allowed to bunch together in one lane. An Olympic track is 400 m long, so in the longer events the athletes run round again and again.

Hurdles, steeplechases and relays

Hurdlers and steeplechasers must jump hurdles as they race. Some of the steeplechase hurdles have pools of water in front of them, and landing in the water will slow down an athlete, so the steeplechasers need to clear the hurdle and the pool. Track relay events have four runners in a team. Each one takes a turn at running with a baton. They must hand the baton over to the next athlete in a 20-m-long changeover box marked on the track, but if they make a mistake they will be out of the race.

Amazing Olympics

In the Paralympics, there are different track event categories including wheelchair races and events for runners with amputated limbs or visual impairment.

Olympic facts and stats

All track races are run anti-clockwise. Each race can have one false start, and then anyone who false starts after that is disqualified (banned from the race).

The longest Olympic running race is the marathon, at over 42 km. It is run on roads outside the Olympic Stadium.

The longest Olympic race of all is the 50-km men's walk.

FIELD EVENTS

Field events are held in the middle of the Olympic Stadium. They include jumping competitions, throwing events and combined events which include a mixture of sports such as throwing, jumping and running.

The jumping events include the high jump, long jump, triple jump and pole vault. The high jumpers must clear a bar that gets gradually higher during the competition. The pole vaulters sprint towards the high bar, plant their pole and try to spring over it. If the high jumpers or pole vaulters knock the bar off three times at the same height they get knocked out of the competition. The long jumpers sprint along a runway and leap into a sandpit from the front of a take-off board. If their take-off foot goes over the front of the board, the judges wave a red flag and the jump doesn't count. The triple-jumpers take a long hop and a step before they jump over the sandpit.

Throwing events

The throwing events include the discus, hammer, shot put and javelin. These sports are amongst the oldest in Olympic history. The ancient Greeks, who invented the Olympic Games in

Australian Steve Hooker goes clear on his way to winning the men's pole vault gold medal at Beijing in 2008.

776 BCE, threw spears and the discus in their competitions. When they are throwing, the competitors must stay inside a specially marked area.

Combined events

The Olympic combined events are the decathlon for men, the heptathlon for women and the modern pentathlon. Decathletes compete in ten different field and track sports in two days. The overall winner is the athlete with the most points. The heptathletes try seven events over two days, and the modern pentathlon competitors have just one day to combine a 3-km-cross-country run with shooting, fencing, swimming and horseriding events.

▶ Aksana Miankova from Belarus wins the Beijing Olympics women's hammer gold medal with a new Olympic record distance of 76.34 m.

Olympic facts and stats

Pole vaulting competitions were held in ancient Greece and Crete, where the athletes vaulted over live bulls.

Pole vaulters used to be able to climb up their poles as they jumped, but this is now against the rules.

Throwing equipment, such as shots, discus and hammers, are heavier for the men's events than for the women's.

Ancient Greek Olympic long jumpers carried weights in their hands as they jumped. This helped propel them forward, so they may have jumped further than today's athletes.

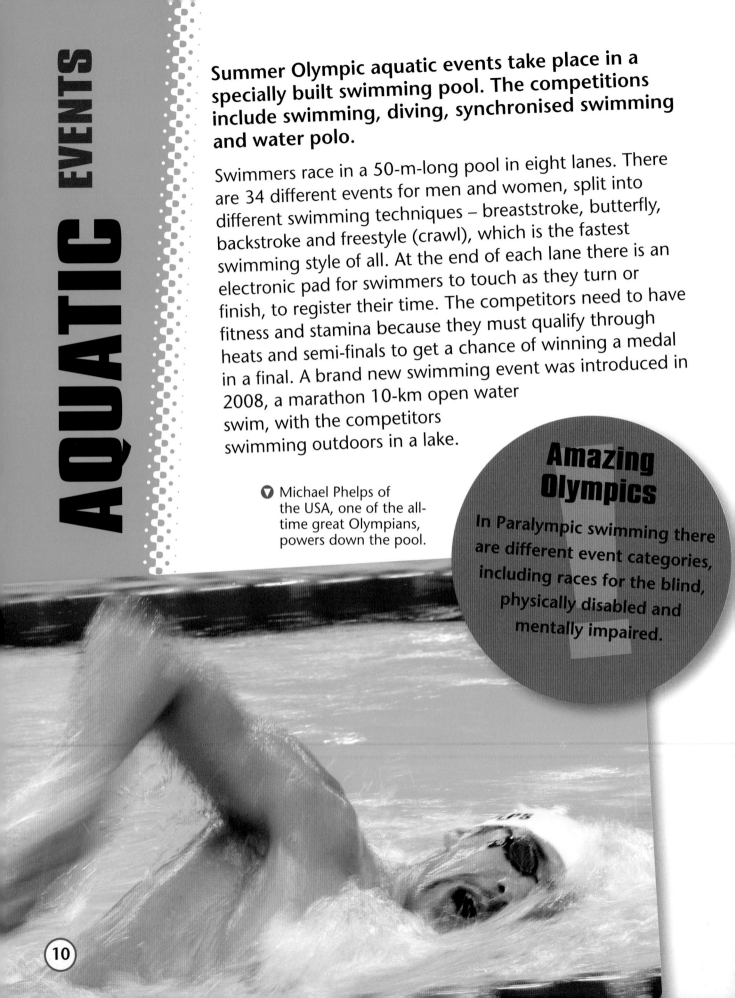

Summer Olympic aquatic events take place in a specially built swimming pool. The competitions include swimming, diving, synchronised swimming and water polo.

Swimmers race in a 50-m-long pool in eight lanes. There are 34 different events for men and women, split into different swimming techniques – breaststroke, butterfly, backstroke and freestyle (crawl), which is the fastest swimming style of all. At the end of each lane there is an electronic pad for swimmers to touch as they turn or finish, to register their time. The competitors need to have fitness and stamina because they must qualify through heats and semi-finals to get a chance of winning a medal in a final. A brand new swimming event was introduced in 2008, a marathon 10-km open water swim, with the competitors swimming outdoors in a lake.

Michael Phelps of the USA, one of the all-time great Olympians, powers down the pool.

Amazing Olympics

In Paralympic swimming there are different event categories, including races for the blind, physically disabled and mentally impaired.

Diving events

There are events for single divers and synchronised diving competitions. There are several different types of dive, including forwards and backwards dives, twisting dives and even a dive that begins with a handstand. Some events take place on the springboard, others take place on a high dive platform. Judges score the dives out of ten.

Synchronised swimming and water polo

There are team and individual womens' synchronised swimming events. Judges score the swimmers on technical moves and artistic performance set to music. There are 20 basic positions and some of them are performed completely underwater. Water polo is fast-moving and noisy. Teams of seven players play in a pitch marked out with floating buoys and goals on a swimming pool. The players must use one hand to throw a ball into the goal.

In the synchronised dives, the two divers try to dive in perfect time with each other.

A goalkeeper looks on anxiously as a shot comes in during the Beijing water polo competition.

Olympic facts and stats

Open water marathon swimmers can be booked like footballers. They get a yellow card for bad behaviour, followed by a red card that disqualifies them.

The synchronised swimming pool has underwater speakers, so the performers can hear the music underwater.

Any Olympic swimmer who false starts is immediately disqualified.

Blind Paralympic swimmers have a 'tapper', a person that taps them with a pole to let them know they are nearing the end of the pool.

EVENTS

The Olympic Equestrian (riding) programme includes three different types of event – show-jumping, eventing and dressage. Men and women compete together in individual and team competitions.

At the Olympic show-jumping arena there are individual and team events. The horses must ride round a course laid out with jumping fences, gates and water jumps. Some of the fences are in rows of two or three. The riders pick up penalty points if they knock down fence poles, refuse to jump, put a hoof in a water jump, go the wrong way or take too long. Both the riders and the horses have to be calm and clever to cope with the challenges.

A show-jumper clears a jump in the 2008 Olympic show-jumping arena.

▶ In dressage, a rider whose horse looks happy and alert gets more points than one whose horse looks tense.

Dressage

The dressage event is a very precise display of horsemanship. It's like a complicated dance, designed to demonstrate how good a horse is at responding to its rider's commands. It has to go through a series of set movements including cantering, trotting and different types of walk. Judges watch carefully and mark each performance out of ten, for technique and elegance.

Eventing

In the eventing competition the riders take part in four events over three days – dressage, cross-country and two rounds of show-jumping. The 6-km-cross-country course is one of the toughest challenges in the whole of the Summer Olympics, with water-filled ditches, streams, and high fences to jump at a gallop. The horses must be strong and the riders fearless, but they also need to be able to do the precise movements of dressage.

Amazing Olympics

Horses are flown to the Olympic host city in passenger jets, in adapted areas of the aeroplane hold. Specially-trained 'flight grooms' look after them on the flights.

Olympic facts and stats

Olympic horses are tested for illegal performance-enhancing drugs, just like human athletes.

Athletes in the modern pentathlon (see page 9) are lent a horse for their show-jumping round and have just 20 minutes to get to know it.

The word 'dressage' comes from the French 'dresser', which means 'to train'. The technique was once used for training cavalry horses in the army.

There were horse-drawn chariot races at the ancient Greek Olympics.

CYCLING EVENTS

There are four different Olympic cycling categories – track cycling, road racing, mountain biking and BMX racing. The track cycling takes place in a specially built velodrome – an arena with an oval-shaped, sloped wooden racing track.

There are ten different track cycling competitions for men and women. The fastest races are the sprints, where riders play a slow-cycling game of cat and mouse for two laps and then explode at speeds up to 96 km/h on the final lap, trying to catch each other by surprise. In the team cycling events you will see riders in a team taking it in turns to ride in front, trying to outwit their opponents. The longest and most complicated team race is the Madison, when teams of two riders take turns riding over a marathon 200 laps, winning points for their position every 20 laps.

Amazing Olympics

The velodrome track has lines on it. The red line is for overtaking, the black line shows the shortest route and the blue line marks where team cyclists can take a break.

Cyclists in the Olympic velodrome power around the track's banked (sloped) sides.

Mountain bikes have to be tough to survive a rugged off-road track.

On-road and off-road events

Road cyclists race over a course of 239 km (for men) or 120 km (for women), or they take part in time trials against the clock. It usually takes about six hours for the men to complete the road race, and between three and four hours for the women. Meanwhile the mountain bikers are tested on a tough off-road course in the countryside, racing each other or by doing time trials over a rough and hilly track. They 'bunny-hop' (jump the bike) over branches, rocks and streams, or get off the bike and run with it over the steepest parts of the course.

BMX

An exciting new Olympic sport, BMX bike racing, was introduced at the Beijing Olympics in 2008. Eight riders race as fast as they can over a dirt track littered with jumps, bumps and tight corners. They fly through the air, launching themselves off the obstacles as they try to overtake their opponents. Each race lasts for just 40 seconds of fast and furious action.

In BMX racing the riders must race while coping with sharp turns and jumps on the course.

Olympic facts and stats

Olympic mountain bikers have to carry their own toolkit, in case they need to make quick repairs during races.

At the first ever modern Olympic Games, held in Greece in 1896, just six riders competed in the cycling road race.

In the Keirin track race the cyclists ride behind a motorbike, which gradually speeds up in front of them.

The cycling sprinters are only timed over the last 200 m of their race.

TARGET SHOOTING

Target shooting events at the Summer Olympics include competitions using airguns, pistols, rifles or arrows. In the Winter Olympics the biathlon combines cross-country skiing with rifle shooting.

There are 15 gun shooting events for men and women, using various different pistols or rifles. In some of the competitions the shooters aim at electronic targets marked with ten circles, each one scoring differently. They must concentrate hard to fire a set amount of shots in a limited time. The fastest competitors are in the rapid-fire pistol events, where they have just a few seconds to fire at a row of five targets. In skeet and trap shooting the competitors aim at saucer-shaped targets shot into the air by a machine. They have to have very fast reactions to hit the discs as they speed across the sky.

Archery events
In the archery competitions the target is 1.22 m wide, but looks tiny to an archer standing 70 m away – about the same size as a drawing pin held at arm's length. The target has ten rings, with a bullseye 12.2 cm

◭ Competitors in trap shooting wear padded vests to protect them from the recoil of the gun.

▶ Three South Korean women archers at a media event demonstrate the strength needed to draw an Olympic bow.

wide. Green and red lights tell them when they can shoot and when their time is up, and they have 15 seconds to load an arrow, aim and fire.

Shooting from skis

In the Winter Olympic biathlon events competitors must complete a tough cross-country ski race, carrying a rifle on their back, before they reach the shooting range. There they must drop their ski poles and take five shots at a target 50 m away. They must do their best to get their heart rate down after the skiing, to give themselves a better chance to shoot accurately. They do this by deep breathing and concentrating hard. If a skier misses a target, minutes are added on to their overall race time. The winner is the competitor who finishes in the shortest time.

A competitor in the Winter Olympics biathlon takes aim through a high-power telescopic sight.

Olympic facts and stats

Shooting and archery competitors have to qualify through different rounds to get to medal finals.

Biathlon ski rifles have special mechanisms fitted on the end to stop them getting blocked with snow.

The string of an Olympic archery bow is stronger than steel.

Olympic archers must bring their own arrows, with their name written on each one.

COMBAT SPORTS

Summer Olympic combat sports include boxing, fencing, judo, taekwondo and wrestling. They are contested with knockout bouts between two opponents, with the winner going through to another round or winning a medal.

The boxing events are organised by weight categories – so the heaviest or lightest people fight against each other. Judges keep a score as they watch the fight, and the winner either has the highest score at the end of four rounds, or knocks out his opponent. There are two different types of Olympic wrestling – freestyle and Greco-Roman. Wrestling and boxing were part of the ancient Olympics but were much more violent and could even result in death.

Amazing Olympics

Paralympic combat sports include judo for the visually impaired and wheelchair fencing. With the wheelchairs fixed to the floor, the fencers concentrate solely on swordplay.

Wrestling was one of the original contests at the ancient Olympic Games.

▶ Fists and feet fly as the competitors try to land scoring blows in taekwondo.

Judo

Judo contestants fight on a foam mat, wearing loose-fitting judo uniforms called 'judogi'. A referee and two judges watch as each contestant tries to score an 'ippon', the judo version of a knockout, by throwing his or her opponent onto their back. In taekwondo, the fighters wear helmets and padding, and their sport is scored by the number of jabs, punches and kicks they land. Contestants shout a loud cry, a 'kiap', every time they try a move.

Fencing

Olympic fencers use three different types of sword – the foil, epee or sabre. They all have different kinds of handle and different fighting rules. Before each bout the fighters salute each other with their swords. Then a referee shouts, "On-guard!" and the bout begins. The fighters must stay inside an area called the 'piste', trying to touch each other with the tips of their swords.

▼ The tips of the fencing swords are wired electronically to register a hit when they touch.

Olympic facts and stats

In ancient Greece, any illegal wrestling moves were punished with a whipping from the referee.

Olympic boxers are not allowed to have beards.

In 2012 there will be boxing events for women for the first time in Olympic history.

During fights judo referees shout 'begin' and 'finish' in Japanese, whereas taekwondo referees shout the same commands in Korean. These countries are where the sports began.

There are lots of team sport events at the Summer Olympics and the Paralympics. They include well-known sports such as football and basketball, and more unusual sports such as beach volleyball and handball.

In Olympic basketball, teams try to score as many baskets as possible against each other, in a timed match. The teams play each other in groups; then the top teams go on to play quarter-finals, semi-finals and finals. Basketball's biggest superstars take part and the matches always have big crowds and millions of TV viewers around the world. Paralympic wheelchair basketball is fast-moving and exciting to watch, too. The players use extra-tough titanium wheelchairs designed to cope with the rough and tumble of the game.

Football

Olympic football teams are allowed three professional players out of eleven. At the 2012 London Olympics the matches will be held in famous football grounds around the UK such as

Sporting superstar Kobe Bryant finds the basket for the USA basketball team.

Old Trafford, home of Manchester United, and Hampden Park, home of the Scottish football team. The Paralympics have five-a-side and seven-a-side football, and the ball has a bell fitted inside it to make a sound that visually-impaired players can hear.

Handball and volleyball

In Olympic handball, teams try to score by throwing a ball at a goal. The best attacking players know how to punch the ball to make it spin and bounce in surprising ways, to fool the goalie. In volleyball and beach volleyball, players use their fists to knock the ball to and fro over a net, trying to keep it going like tennis players. Beach volleyball is played on sand, which makes it harder for players to move around but produces spectacular shots and saves, because the players don't mind falling on the soft sand.

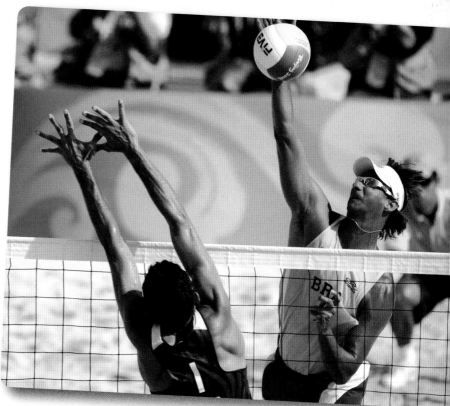

⊙ The beach volleyball court is filled with sand to replicate beach conditions.

Amazing Olympics

A new team sport, seven-a-side rugby for men and women, will be part of the Rio De Janeiro Olympics in 2016.

Olympic facts and stats

Paralympic players take part in sitting volleyball, using only their upper bodies to reach the ball.

At the London Olympics in 2012 the beach volleyball competition will be held on a fake beach at Horseguards Parade, near Downing Street in Whitehall, central London.

One of the greatest Olympic team medal runs ever was in field hockey, when the Indian team won every gold medal in men's hockey between 1928 and 1956.

In Paralympic football for the visually impaired, all the players wear eye masks, to make sure that nobody can see better than anybody else.

SPORTS

Badminton, tennis and table tennis are all part of the Summer Olympics. They are played in individual or team competitions.

Tennis includes men's and women's singles and doubles, played in knockout competitions. At the 2012 London Olympics the competitions will be played on the world-famous grass courts of Wimbledon. The world's top-ranking players qualify to take part, and some of the greatest ever players have won Olympic gold, including Rafa Nadal (men's singles champion 2008) and Venus Williams (2000 ladies singles champion and 2008 doubles champion with her sister Serena). Tennis is played at the Paralympics, too, in wheelchair events.

Badminton

Badminton has men's and women's singles and doubles competitions. It is played on an indoor court with a net higher than a standard tennis net, lightweight rackets and a shuttlecock made of bird feathers. It first became an Olympic sport in 1992, and so far Asian countries have

◭ Spain's Rafa Nadal keeps his eye on the ball en route to the 2008 Olympic men's tennis gold medal.

◀ China's Lin Dan, men's badminton gold medallist in 2008, leaps to smash the shuttlecock.

been the most successful. China does extremely well at badminton, with a record 30 medals, 11 of them gold.

Table tennis

Men and women play singles and team events in Olympic table tennis competitions. The sport is very fast and needs good agility, quick reflexes and great hand-eye co-ordination. The best players use different techniques to make the ball spin, so it shoots in surprising ways as it bounces. They use wooden bats with a rubber covering, which they glue on only minutes before a match, to ensure the very best bat performance.

Amazing Olympics

All Olympic sports have their own pictogram – a picture symbol used to represent them on posters and signs at the Games.

⬥ Most of the best Olympic table tennis players are from Asian countries, where they are sporting superstars.

Olympic facts and stats

The first-ever tennis gold medallist was an Irish student who won the men's event in Athens in 1896. He just came to watch the Olympics, and only decided to enter after he arrived.

Tennis players who win at the Olympics get points towards their world ranking, helping them to qualify for other competitions around the world.

Table tennis is also called ping-pong or whiff-whaff. It is a Paralympic wheelchair event.

Table tennis began in the 1800s, when wealthy people played it after formal dinner, using champagne corks as balls and cigar boxes as bats.

BOAT SPORTS

Rowing, canoeing and sailing take place on lakes or on the coast of the Summer Olympic host country.

The Olympic rowing course is set out in a lake, with six lanes marked by buoys on the water. There are 14 different rowing events for men and women, using different-sized boats. Crews are either singles, pairs, fours or eights. They must be super-fit and have lots of stamina to keep going to the end of the race. In sculling events each rower has two oars. In sweep races each rower has one oar. The biggest boats are for the eights – eight rowers and a coxswain, who shouts at the rowers to help them keep their rhythm and encourage them to keep trying.

⬢ Team Australia rowing coxless four at Beijing in 2008.

Sailing events

There are ten sailing events for men and women, in different boat classes (types of boat). These include dinghies, keelboats (sailing boats), multihulls (boats with more than one hull, such as catamarans) and windsurfers. The competitors sail around a course marked out with buoys.

◀ Great Britain's Ben Ainslie wins gold for the fourth time in the Finn Olympic sailing class in Beijing.

They take part in several rounds, collecting points for their position as they cross the finish line. The winner collects the least points overall. The sailors need skill and strength to get round the course, setting their sails to get the maximum speed and power from the wind.

Canoeing events

There are two types of canoe event at the Olympics – slalom and sprint. A slalom competition is a timed run down a rough, swirling, white water course with obstacles, steep drops and fast currents. There are up to 25 gates to get through, but touching or missing out a gate incurs time penalties. The sprint canoeists race in lanes across calm water, at 200 m, 500 m or 1,000 m. Some canoeists compete in kayaks, sitting down in the boat and using a paddle with a blade on both sides. Others compete in a canoe, kneeling and using a paddle which has a blade on one side.

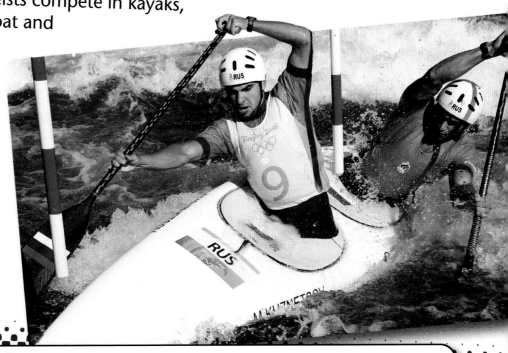

▷ The slalom doubles requires great strength, skill and teamwork to avoid touching the gates.

Olympic facts and stats

Rowing is the only sport where the competitors cross the line backwards.

Coxswains are weighed before they race. If they are lighter than other coxswains in the competition the judges will add weights to their boat to even up the competition.

At the Athens Olympics in 1906 there was a rowing race with 17-man crews.

Olympic windsurfers must all use the same brand of windsurfing equipment, chosen by the IOC, to make sure the competition is fair.

TECHNIQUE

Gymnastics and weight-lifting are both Olympic categories that require super-fitness and many hours of highly-focused training to get the technique exactly right.

Artistic gymnastics is a category of events that uses apparatus or a floor mat. The apparatus includes bars, rings, a vault or a pommel horse, which all need lots of body strength and amazing balance. In the floor exercises competitors have 70 seconds to combine a sequence of jumps, somersaults and twists, which are scored by the judges. In rhythmic gymnastics events the competitors perform floor routines to music using equipment, which could be a hoop, ribbon, ball, rope or club. Judges watch all the performances and score them on technique, difficulty and style. Any slight error could end a medal chance.

◀ Romania's Nadia Comãneci performs a floor routine at Montreal in 1976.

Amazing Olympics

Nadia Comãneci made history at the 1976 Olympics in Montreal, when she scored the first ever perfect 10 given in a gymnastics competition, for her routine on the uneven bars.

Trampolining

The newest gymnastics sport is trampolining, introduced in 2000. The competitors bounce up to 10 m high, doing somersaults, twists and backflips to earn marks from the judges. Sequences of trampoline somersaults and twists have special names, including the rudolph, cat leap and fliffi. The judges give high scores for style and technique and for landing accurately back on the trampoline.

Weight-lifting

There are 15 weight-lifting events for men and women, organised in different classes based on the bodyweight of the competitors. The weight-lifters must hoist a barbell, a metal bar loaded with weighted discs on either end. More discs are gradually added to make the barbell heavier. There are two kinds of lifts. In a 'clean and jerk', the weight-lifter lifts the barbell to his shoulders while squatting, then stands up and lifts the barbell overhead. In a 'snatch' lift, the weight-lifter starts the move standing, then lifts the barbell up. The referees judge if the lifts have been done correctly; otherwise they don't count.

⬥ Latvia's Viktors Scerbatihs wins bronze in the men's super-heavyweight weight-lifting competition.

Olympic facts and stats

Male Olympic gymnasts don't have music for their floor exercises, but women do.

Rope-climbing was once an Olympic gymnastics event. It was scored by the height the climbers achieved and for their climbing style.

Weight-lifters wear special weight-lifting shoes that help them to grip the floor as they lift.

In Paralympic power-lifting the competitors lie down and push the barbell upwards.

WINTER OLYMPICS

The Winter Olympics, held every four years, attracts the best winter sports athletes in the world. Categories include skiing, ice hockey, curling, luge, bobsleigh and ice-skating.

Ski events include alpine (downhill) skiing, cross-country skiing, freestyle skiing and snowboarding. Alpine skiers ski as fast as they can down a hillside course. Cross-country skiers trek over a countryside course. Freestyle skiing includes exciting mogul competitions, when skiers race down a bumpy track or perform tricks over the bumps (called moguls). Ski-cross and snowboard-cross are exciting fast-moving races between four competitors, while the aerial skiing and snowboard halfpipe events produce breathtaking acrobatics that are scored by watching judges.

Luge and bobsleigh

The luge and bobsleigh competitions are the super-fast events of the Winter Olympics. Lugers lie on their backs on a sled, steering it by moving their body as

Hannah Teter of the United States competes in the snowboard womens' halfpipe, Vancouver, 2010.

they hurtle down an icy track at up to 150 km/h, with no brakes. Bobsleigh teams of two or four jump into a bobsleigh shaped like a rocket, with brakes and steering pulleys, and race around a course at up to 150 km/h. The skeleton bobsleighers lie on their stomachs on a sled that looks like a large tea tray with handles, reaching speeds of up to 135 km/h as they shoot down the track.

🔵 Shen Xue and Xao Honbo win gold for China in the pairs figure-skating competition in Vancouver, 2010.

On the ice

Indoor Winter Olympic events include curling, ice hockey and ice-skating. Curling and ice hockey are both exciting tense knockout team competitions. Ice hockey is a fast all-action sport that needs bravery and quick reactions, while curling needs concentration to make accurate shots. As individuals or pairs, ice skaters perform to music and are scored by judges for technique and artistic skill.

Amazing Olympics

The Winter Olympics and the Summer Olympics take place two years apart. The next Winter Olympics will be held in 2014, in Sochi, Russia.

Olympic facts and stats

The Winter Paralympics take place immediately after the Winter Olympics, in the same venue. They include ice sledge hockey and wheelchair curling.

Lugers wear gloves fitted with sharp 4-mm-spikes, to help them push on the ice at the beginning of a run.

Bobsleighers and lugers wear helmets like motor racing drivers, along with tight-fitting aerodynamic suits.

Ski jumpers launch themselves from a high ramp, hitting speeds above 90 km/h as they reach the end of the ramp.

GLOSSARY

Barbell A metal bar with weighted plates fitted on either end, for weight-lifters to raise up.

Biathlon An event that combines a cross-country skiing race with a shooting competition.

Bullseye The centre of a shooting or archery target. Hitting the bullseye scores the highest amount of points.

Compulsory round A performance in which a competitor must do certain set moves.

Coxswain Someone who sits in the back of a rowing boat facing the front, steering and keeping the oarsmen or women rowing together.

Decathlon An event for men that consists of ten different sports. Competitors build up a score as they take part in each one.

Dressage A series of very precise movements made by a horse and controlled by a rider.

Equestrian events Horseriding competitions.

Field events Events that take place in the centre of the main Olympic stadium, such as throwing and jumping events.

Freestyle An event where competitors can perform their own unique routine.

Halfpipe A U-shaped track used for snowboarding performances.

Heptathlon An event for women that consists of seven sports.

Hurdles Jumps placed on the athletics running track, for hurdling and steeplechase events.

IOC International Olympic Committee, the organisation that runs the Olympic Games.

Judges Experts who give scores to Olympic competitors in sports such as gymnastics and ice-dancing.

Lanes Separate routes for each competitor, marked on a track or in a swimming pool.

Long-distance running Races of 5,000 m or 10,000 m.

Marathon A long-distance running race that takes place through the streets of the host city during the Summer Olympics.

Middle-distance running Races of 800 m and 1,500 m.

Modern pentathlon An event that consists of five different sports.

Mogul A man-made bump on a snowy track.

Olympian Someone who has competed in the Olympics.

Paralympics Summer and Winter Olympic Games held every four years for disabled athletes.

Performance-enhancing drugs Drugs taken to make an athlete perform better (also called 'doping').

Pictogram A picture symbol given to every Olympic sport.

Red flag Waved by a judge if a long or triple jumper steps too far forwards before jumping.

Skeet A shooting event, where competitors fire at clay disks shot into the air.

Slalom A course where a competitor must weave round poles or go through gates, used in skiing and canoeing.

Sprinter A fast runner who competes in short races of 100 m, 200 m or 400 m.

Steeplechase A running race where athletes have to jump hurdles, some with water-filled ditches behind them.

Synchronised Where a team performs exactly the same moves at the same time, such as in synchronised diving and swimming.

Track events Athletics events that are run around the track in the main Olympic Stadium.

Velodrome Cycling arena.

Youth Olympics Summer and Winter Olympic Games held every four years for athletes aged between 14 and 18.

LIST OF OLYMPIC EVENTS

Summer Olympics

Aquatics (swimming pool sports)

Archery

Athletics

Badminton

Basketball

Boxing

Canoeing

Cycling

Equestrian (horseriding)

Fencing

Football

Gymnastics

Handball

Hockey

Judo

Modern pentathlon

Rowing

Sailing

Shooting

Table tennis

Taekwondo

Tennis

Trampolining

Triathlon

Volleyball

Weight-lifting

Wrestling

Winter Olympics

Biathlon

Bobsleigh

Curling

Ice hockey

Ice skating

Luge

Skiing (alpine, cross-country)

Summer Paralympics

Archery

Athletics

Boccia

Cycling

Equestrian

Football (5-a-side, 7-a-side)

Goalball

Judo

Powerlifting

Rowing

Sailing

Shooting

Swimming

Table tennis

Volleyball

Wheelchair basketball

Wheelchair fencing

Wheelchair rugby

Wheelchair tennis

Winter Paralympics

Biathlon

Cross-country skiing

Ice sledge hockey

Skiing (alpine, cross-country)

Wheelchair curling

Useful Olympic websites

www.olympic.org The official website of the Olympic Movement.

www.olympic.org.uk Official website for the British Olympic teams.

www.london2012.com The official website of the London Summer Olympics, 2012.

www.paralympics.org The official website of the Paralympics.

www.bbc.co.uk/history/greeks/greek_olympics Find out about the history of the Ancient Greek Games.

INDEX

Here are the lists of contents for each title in *The Olympics*...

History
The birth of the Olympics • Olympics reborn • Faster, higher, stronger
Hard times and heroes • Cold War Olympics • Sporting Sixties
Triumphs and disaster • TV Times • New teams, new hope
Hi-tech, high cost • The 2012 Olympics • Olympic future

Scandals
All about the Olympics • Ancient trouble • New games, new problems
Money vs love • Politics wins • Protests and tragedy • Bribes for votes
Doping to win • Caught! • Cheating one-offs
Medical matters • Future shocks

Events
All about the Olympics • Track events • Field events • Aquatic events
Equestrian events • Cycling events • Target shooting
Combat sports • Summer team sports • Racket sports • Boat sports
Strength and technique • Winter Olympics

Records
All about Olympic records • Fastest men
Fastest women • Highest and longest • Super-strongest
Endurance records • In it together – team sports
Water golds • Bullseye champions • Scoring high
Paralympic record-breakers • In the snow